Compiled by Emma van Dodeweerd

TOP THAT! Kids™

Published by Top That! Publishing plc
Tide Mill Way, Woodbridge, Suffolk, IP12 1AP, UK
www.topthatpublishing.com

Why didn't the monster use toothpaste?

Because he said his teeth weren't loose.

Did you hear about the monster who sent his picture to a lonely hearts club?

They sent it back saying they weren't that lonely.

What happened when the monster fell down the well?

He kicked the bucket.

Why are a monster's fingers never more than 11 inches long?

Because if they were 12 inches, they would be a foot!

What game do monsters play with ants?

Squash!

What do you call a yeti in a phone box?

Stuck.

What is a sea monster's favourite dish?

Fish and ships.

What happened when the nasty monster stole a pig?

The pig squealed to the police.

Did
you hear about the
monster who lost all his
hair in the war?

He lost it in a hair-raid.

Where do abominable snowmen
go to dance?

To snowballs.

Why was the sword-swallowing
monster put in prison?

He coughed and killed two people.

How do you know when there's
a monster under your bed?

Your nose touches the ceiling.

What did the big, hairy monster do when he lost a hand?

He went to the second-hand shop.

Why was the monster standing on his head?

He was turning things over in his mind.

What is the best way to get rid of a demon?

Exorcise a lot!

Why did the two cyclops fight?

They could never see eye to eye over anything.

Why did the monster cross the road?

He wanted to know what it felt like to be a chicken.

Why was the big, hairy, two-headed monster top of the class at school?

Because two heads are better than one.

Why did the cyclops give up teaching?

Because he only had one pupil.

How does a yeti get to work?

By icicle!

How can you tell the difference between a monster and a banana?

Try picking it up. If you can't, it's either a monster or a giant banana.

Monster 1: "I've just changed my mind."

Monster 2: "Does it work any better?"

Why did the monster say he was an actor?

His leg was in a cast.

Did the bionic monster have a brother?

No, but he had lots of trans-sisters!

What is a monster after it is five years old?

Six years old.

What do you get if you cross a man-eating monster with a skunk?

A very ugly smell.

Did you hear about the monster burglar who fell in the cement mixer?

He is now a hardened criminal.

Did you hear about the monster who was known as Captain Kirk?

He had a left ear, a right ear and a final front ear.

What happened when the
ice monster ate a curry?

He blew his cool.

Where
does a big, hairy monster sleep?

Anywhere he wants to.

Monster 1: "That gorgeous four-eyed
creature just rolled her eyes at me!"

Monster 2: "Well roll them back again.
She might need them!"

How did the monster cure his sore throat?

He spent all day gargoyling.

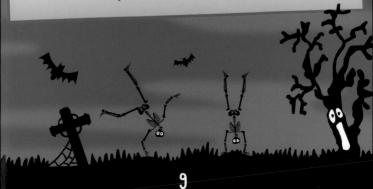

Did you hear about the monster who had eight arms?

He said they came in handy.

What do you get if a huge hairy monster steps on Batman and Robin?

Flatman and Ribbon!

What did the angry monster do when he got his gas bill?

He exploded.

The police are looking for a monster with one eye.

Why don't they use two?

Did you hear about the monster with one eye at the back of his head and one eye at the front of his head?

He was terribly moody because he couldn't see eye to eye with anyone.

What do you call a monster who sleeps on your doorstep?

Matt.

Why did the monster have to buy two tickets to the zoo?

He needed one to get in and one to get out!

What business is King Kong in?

Monkey business.

What do abominable monsters call their offspring?

Chill-dren.

On which day do monsters eat people?

Chewsday!

How does a monster make toast?

He puts it under a gorilla.

Why do monsters have lots of matted fur?

Because they'd look silly in plastic macs.

Why did the monster drink ten litres of anti-freeze?

So that he didn't have to buy a winter coat.

Which monster is the unluckiest monster in the world?

The Luck Less Monster.

What does a polite monster say when he meets someone for the first time?

Pleased to eat you!

What kind of monster can sit on the end of your finger?

The bogeyman.

What do you give a monster with big feet?

Big flippers.

What did one of the monster's eyes say to the other?

Between us is something that smells.

How do you greet a three-headed monster?

Hello, hello, hello.

Why are monsters covered in wrinkles?

Have you ever tried to iron a monster?

What
do you do with a
blue monster?

Try to cheer him up!

What is big, hairy and bounces
up and down?

A monster on a pogo stick.

How can you tell the
difference between a rabbit
and a red-eyed monster?

Just try getting a red-eyed
monster into a rabbit hutch.

Why couldn't Swamp Thing go
to the party?

Because he was bogged down at work!

What should you do if a monster runs through your front door?

Run through the back door.

What's the hardest part of making monster soup?

Stirring it!

What steps should you take if a monster is following you?

Very large ones!

Teacher: "What can you tell me about the dinosaurs?"

Pupil: "They're all dead."

What's
blue and hairy and
goes round and round?

A monster on a
merry-go-round.

Why did the wooden monsters
stand in a circle?

They were having a board meeting.

What do you get if you cross
the Loch Ness Monster with a shark?

Lock Jaws.

What
do you get if you
cross an abominable monster
with an elephant?

A jumbo yeti.

What happens if a big, hairy monster sits in front of you at the cinema?

You miss most of the film!

What do you do with a green monster?

Put him in the sun until he ripens.

What did the monster say when he saw a rush-hour train full of passengers?

"Oh good! A chew-chew train!"

How do you address a monster?

Very politely.

What do you get if you cross a tall, green monster with a fountain pen?

The Ink-credible Hulk.

Little Monster: "Mum I've finished. Can I leave the table?"

Mummy Monster: "Yes, I'll save it for your tea."

Why did the monster eat a light bulb?

Because he was in need of light refreshment.

What does a monster mum say to her kids at dinner time?

"Don't talk with someone in your mouth."

What happened to Ray
when he met the
man-eating monster?

He became an ex-Ray!

Who
won the Monster
Beauty Contest?

No one.

Why do waiters prefer monsters
to flies?

Have you ever heard anyone complaining
of a monster in their soup?

Monster: "Doctor, doctor, how do
I stop my nose from running?"

Doctor: "Stick your foot out and
trip it up."

What's
a giant's favourite
tale?

A tall story.

How do you know if a monster
is musical?

He's got a flat head.

What did the monster say when
he saw Snow White and the
Seven Dwarfs?

"Yum, Yum!"

What
time is it when a
monster sits on your car?

Time to get a new car.

Monster: "Doctor, doctor, how long can one live without a brain?"

Doctor: "That depends. How old are you?"

What do skeletons have nightmares of?

Dogs!

What kind of monster has the best hearing?

The eeriest.

What happened to the evil monster that fell in the marmalade jar?

Nothing, he was a jammy devil!

What did the shy pebble monster say?

I wish I was a little boulder.

Monster: "Doctor, doctor, what did the x-ray of my head show?"

Doctor: "Absolutely nothing."

What happened when the monster stole a bottle of perfume?

He was convicted of fragrancy.

Did you hear about the monster who had an extra pair of hands?

He kept them in a handbag.

What is as big as the Abominable Snow Monster but doesn't weigh anything?

His shadow.

Why did the monster cross the road?

He was dressed up as a chicken.

What is the smelliest, hairiest monarch in the world?

King Pong!

Why did the monster paint himself in rainbow colours?

Because he wanted to hide in the crayon box.

Did you hear about the monster who went to a holiday camp?

He won the ugly mug and knobbly knees competition and he wasn't even entered.

What do you get if a monster sits on your best mate?

A flat mate.

What do you get if you cross King Kong with a watchdog?

A terrified postman.

Where did the flying mammoth land?

At the earport.

What do you get if you cross a plum with a man-eating monster?

A purple people-eater.

What's big, heavy, furry, dangerous and has sixteen wheels?

A monster on roller skates.

Did you hear about the monsters that got engaged?

It was love at first fright!

What Scottish monster is always untidy?

The Loch Mess monster.

What's
big, red and prickly, has
three eyes and eats rocks?

A big, red, prickly, three-eyed
rock-eating monster.

What do you get if you cross a
prehistoric monster with a sleeper?

A dinosnore!

What's the difference between a
monster and a biscuit?

You can't dunk a monster in your tea!

What do you call an angry monster?

Sir.

Why did the little monster only wear one boot?

Because it heard that the snow was one foot deep.

What do you call a flea that lives in a monster's ear?

A space invader!

Boy monster: "You've got a face like a million dollars."

Girl monster: "Have I really?"

Boy monster: "Yes, it's green and wrinkly."

What kind of pasta does the Abominable Monster like best?

Spa-yeti!

What do you give a seasick monster?

Plenty of room.

What is a baby monster's favourite nursery rhyme?

Little Bo Creep.

Why can't you put a monster in a sandwich?

It's too heavy to lift.

How does Frankenstein's monster sit?

Bolt upright.

What does a scary monster have for breakfast?

Dreaded wheat.

What do you call a sweet, pleasant, good-natured monster?

A failure.

Girl monster: "Will you still love me when I am old and ugly?"

Boy monster: "Of course I do."

What was the first thing the monster ate when he got his new false teeth?

The dentist.

What do monsters do
with cannonballs?

Play marbles.

How did the ghost get into
the house?

It used a skeleton key.

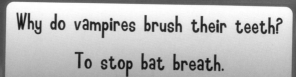

What did one ghost say to the
other ghost?

"Do you believe in people?"

Why do vampires brush their teeth?

To stop bat breath.

What should
a short-sighted
ghost have?

Spooktacles.

When do ghosts
play tricks on each other?

On April Ghoul's Day.

What
haunts an operating
theatre?

Surgical spirits.

What room makes
zombies nervous?

The living room.

How do you make a
skeleton laugh?

Tickle its funny bone.

How do you stop a werewolf
attacking you?

Throw a stick and shout
"Fetch, boy."

What haunts aeroplanes?

High spirits.

Why did Dracula take
some medicine?

To stop his coffin.

What did the vampire say
to his girlfriend?

"Let's go out for a bite."

What
do you get if
you cross Dracula
with Al Capone?

A fangster.

What is a ghost's favourite
entertainment?

Phantomime.

What did the father
ghost say to his son?

"Spook when you're spooken to."

What do vampires have at eleven o'clock every day?

A coffin break.

What's a vampire's favourite sport?

Batminton.

Mummy Monster: "Stop reaching across the table like that. Haven't you got a tongue?"

Little Monster: "Yes, but my arm's longer."

What happened to the two mad vampires?

They both went a little batty.

Why does Dracula have
no friends?

Because he's a pain in the neck.

What
do you call a dog
owned by Dracula?

A blood hound.

What do you call a
demon who slurps his food?

A goblin.

Why are vampire families so close?

Because blood is thicker than water.

Which flavour ice cream is
Dracula's favourite?

Vein-illa.

What
does a headless horseman ride?

A night-mare.

Why was the young
vampire a failure?

Because he fainted at the
sight of blood.

Doctor: "You need new glasses."

Monster: "How did you guess?"

Doctor: "I could tell the moment you
walked through the window."

37

What's a vampire's favourite cartoon character?

Batman.

How do you make a werewolf stew?

Keep him waiting for two hours.

What happened when the werewolf swallowed a clock?

He got ticks.

How do you stop a werewolf howling in the back of a car?

Put him in the front.

What
do foreign devils speak?

Devil Dutch.

What do female monsters look for?

Edible bachelors.

Why did the cyclops apply
for half a television licence?

Because he only had one eye.

What do you get if King
Kong sits on your piano?

A flat note.

What do you get if you cross
King Kong with a snowman?

Frostbite.

What do you get if you cross King Kong
with a budgie?

A messy cage.

What trees
do ghouls like best?

Ceme-trees.

What do you get if you
cross a monster with a flea?

Lots of worried dogs.

Why are graveyards so noisy?

Because of all the coffin.

Why are ghosts bad
at telling lies?

Because you can see
right through them.

What's brown and furry on the
inside and clear on the outside?

King Kong in clingfilm.

What's
green and wrinkly and
goes up and down?

A monster with
hiccups.

What did the clean
monster say to the insect?

"Long time, no flea!"

What
kind of money do
snow monsters use?

Ice lolly.

What happened to the werewolf
who ate garlic?

His bark was worse than his bite.

Why did the small werewolf bite the
woman's ankle?

Because he couldn't reach any higher.

What do monsters say before telling jokes?

"This will slay you."

What does a monster spider do when he gets angry?

He goes up the wall!

Why does every soccer team have a monster?

Because they all have a ghoulkeeper.

Have you heard about the monster who soaked his top half in candle wax?

He wanted to be wicked!

Have you heard about the monster who fell in love with a bee?

He became a honey monster.

What do ghosts play at parties?

Hide and Shriek, then Haunt the Thimble.

What do you say when a monster gets angry?

"No need to bite my head off!"

What does the Invisible Man call his mum and dad?

Transparents.

What did the monster say to the pig?

"You are such a bore!"

Why can't spectres see very well?

Because they don't wear spectrecals.

What do monsters play at parties?

Swallow my leader.

What do you call a monster who is black and blue all over?

Bruce.

Why shouldn't you keep a two-headed monster?

Because it costs twice as much to feed.

What do you give a monster with big feet?

Plenty of room.

Did you hear about the monster who ate a sofa and two chairs?

He had a suite tooth.

What do you get if you cross a monster with a canary?

A big yellow thing that goes 'tweet'.

What happens when a witch
breaks the sound barrier?

A sonic broom.

What's
big and ugly and has
red spots?

A monster with measles.

Why can't some monsters ski?

Because they are
abominable snowmen.

What's a vampire's favourite pudding?

Leeches and scream.

What has webbed feet and fangs?

Count Quackula.

What's big and green with horns?

A monster marching in a band!

What did the teacher say to the ghost?

"Your son is high-spirited."

What's round and bad tempered?

A vicious circle.

What did the teacher
say to the bogeyman?

"Your son gets right
up my nose."

How
do monsters have
their eggs?

Terri-fried.

What did the teacher say to the
parent monster?

"Your daughter is a little monster."

Why do witches ride
broomsticks?

Because vacuum cleaners haven't
got long enough cords.

Where do monsters go on holiday?

Zombia.

What did the teacher say to the evil monster?

"Your son is a little devil."

Why do monsters have wavy hair?

Because they drink sea water.

Why do monsters frighten kids?

Because if they didn't, they would be on the dole.

What do you get if you cross a monster with a biscuit?

Crumbs.

What's white, woolly and ugly?

A monster in sheep's clothing.

Why do some monsters eat raw meat?

Because they don't know how to cook.

What exams do yetis take?

Snow levels.

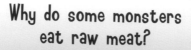

What do you get if you cross a porcupine with a monster?

A huge and ugly toothbrush.

What happened to the cannibal lion?

He had to swallow his pride.

What does a witch do if her broom is stolen?

She calls the Flying Squad.

What's the most dangerous animal in the north?

Yak the ripper!

What
do you get if you cross
a yeti with a kangaroo?

A fur coat with
big pockets.

What's big, black and white and makes
a lot of noise?

A stripy monster with a set of drums.

What makes more noise than an
angry monster?

Two angry monsters.

What
happened when the baby
witch was born?

It was so ugly its parents ran
away from home.

Why did the monster stop playing with his brother?

He got tired of kicking him around.

How do witches on broomsticks drink their tea?

Out of flying saucers.

What do you call a monster who kills his mother and father?

An orphan.

What happened when the monster went for a job as a TV presenter?

The producer said that he had the perfect face for radio.

Where do the cleanest monsters live?

Bath.

What do you call a monster who climbs up walls?

Ivy.

Why did the monster have green ears and a red nose?

So he could hide in the rhubarb patches.

Is it true that a monster won't hurt you if you run away from it?

It all depends on how fast you run!

How can you tell when witches are carrying a time bomb?

You can hear their brooms tick!

What does a monster turn into when the lights go out?

The dark.

What's big, ugly and goes up and down all day?

A monster in a lift.

Who went into the monster's house and came out alive?

The monster.

When a monster falls into a pond, what is the first thing that he does?

Gets wet.

Why don't ant-eating monsters get sick?

Because they're full of anty-bodies.

What do you get if you cross a giant, hairy monster with a penguin?

I don't know but it's a very tight-fitting dinner suit.

Where do you find wild yetis?

It depends where you left them.

What is a ghost's favourite
TV programme?

Horrornation Street.

Why
did Frankenstein squeeze
his girlfriend to death?

He had a crush on her.

What's Dracula's favourite dance?

The fango-dando.

What is Dracula's motto?

The morgue the merrier.

What happened when Dr Frankenstein swallowed some uranium?

He got atomic-ache.

Why is Dracula a good person to take out to dinner?

Because he eats necks to nothing.

What do you get if you cross a bee with a large ape?

Sting Kong.

Was Dracula ever married?

No, he was a bat-chelor.

What do you call the
offspring of a bat and rat?

BRAT!

What's big, ugly, green and red?

A monster with a nappy rash.

Why
is it safe to tell a
mummy your secret?

It'll be kept
under wraps!

What do ghosts put on
their roast beef?

Grave-y.

What do you call a monster with cotton wool in each ear?

Anything you want. He can't hear you!

Ugly monster: "Green hair runs in our family. What runs in yours?"

Bogeyman: "Our noses."

What is a ghost's favourite game?

Corpses and robbers.

Where does a ghost train stop?

At a manifestation.

How did the monster make gold soup?

He put in 24 carrots.

What do you get if you cross a policeman with a ghost?

An inspectre.

How is a cowardly monster like a leaky tap?

They both run.

What do ghosts like to chew?

Boo-ble gum.

What is big, blue
and hairy?

A monster holding its
breath.

Where do you find
monster snails?

At the ends of monsters' fingers.

Why did the monster
give up boxing?

He didn't want to
ruin his looks.

Did
you hear about the witch
who gave birth to identical twins?

She couldn't tell which
was witch.

What's
a vampire's
favourite dance?

The vaults.

Why do monsters
scratch themselves?

Because they're the only ones who know
where they itch.

What's the best way to tell a
monster he's ugly?

Telephone him long distance.

What happened to Frankenstein's
Monster when he was caught speeding?

He was fined £50 and dismantled for
six months.

What part of the
newspaper does Dracula
like best?
The horrorscopes.

What was the inscription on the
tomb of Frankenstein's Monster?

Here lies Frankenstein's Monster.
May he rest in pieces.

What's
the difference between a
monster and peanut butter?

A monster doesn't stick to the
roof of your mouth.

What's the first thing
gorillas learn at school?

Their Ape-B-C.

What's a vampire's favourite soup?

Scream of tomato.

Why did Doctor Frankenstein tiptoe past the medicine cabinet?

He didn't want to wake the sleeping pills.

What's a spook's favourite ride at the amusement park?

The roller ghoster.

What is big, green and squirts jam.

A monster eating a doughnut.

What do devils drink?

Demonade.

What do you find in a zombie's veins?

Dead blood corpuscles.

How do you raise a baby monster that has been abandoned by its parents?

With a fork lift truck.

Who brings the monsters their babies?

Frankenstork.

What did Godzilla have at the 'All you can Eat' restaurant?

The Waiters!

How do you know if a zombie is tired?

He is dead on his feet.

How did Frankenstein's monster eat his lunch?

He bolted it down.

How did the vampire stop his son biting his nails?

He cut all his fingers off.

How do you stop a monster
from smelling?

Cut off his nose.

Did you hear about the
monster that has
pedestrian eyes?

They look both ways before
they cross.

What jewels do
monsters wear?

Tomb stones.

Where
do space monsters live?

In far-off terror-tory.

Did you hear about the girl monster who wasn't pretty and wasn't ugly?

She was pretty ugly.

Which monster made friends with the three bears?

Ghouldilocks.

What is the monster's favourite football team?

Slitherpool.

Monster: "Doctor, doctor, I feel like an invisible monster."

Doctor: "Who said that?"

Why did the monster go
into hospital?

To have his ghoul-stones removed.

Where
does a baby ghost go
while its parents are at work?

Day scare!

What's big and ugly and
takes aspirins?

A monster with a headache.

How many
hairs are in a
monster's tail?

None. They are all on
the outside.

Did you hear about the monster who went on a crash diet?

He wrecked three cars and a bus.

How do you get to the monster's house?

Turn fright at the dead end.

Did you hear about the monster with five legs?

His trousers fit him like a glove.

What's big and ugly and drinks out of the wrong side of the glass?

A monster trying to get rid of hiccups.

Why did the monster dye her hair yellow?

To see if blondes have more fun.

What's big and ugly and goes at 125 mph?

A monster on an Inter-City train.

What's the difference between a monster and a mouse?

A monster makes bigger holes in the skirting board.

What is a monster who is married with seven children called?

DADDY.

If storks bring human babies, what brings monster babies?

Cranes.

How do monsters like their shepherd's pie?

Made with real shepherds.

What is big and hairy and goes beep beep?

A monster in a traffic jam.

What is big and hairy and hangs on the line?

A drip-dry monster.

What is the best way to
see a monster?

On the television.

What is a monster's
favourite society?

The Consumers' Association.

What did the monster eat
at the 'all you can eat'
restaurant?

The waiters!

How do monsters tell the future?

With horrorscopes.

What do you get if you cross a bird with a monstrous snarl?

A budgerigrrrrr!

What do you get if you cross a monster with a pig?

Large pork chops.

What do you get if you cross a monster with a boy scout?

A monster that scares old ladies across the street.

Monster girl: "Mum says that we're having Aunty for Christmas dinner this year."

Monster boy: "Well, she can't possibly be tougher than last year's turkey!"

What do you get if you cross a monster with a kangaroo?

Big holes in Australia.

Monster woman: "I have the face of a sixteen-year-old girl."

Monster boy: "Well you'd better give it back then. You're getting it all wrinkled."

What's green and wrinkled?

The Incredible Hulk's granny.

What's green, seven feet tall and mopes in the corner?

The Incredible Sulk.

How do you get a monster into a matchbox?

Take all the matches out first.

What happened to the monster who ran away with the circus?

The police made him bring it back.

Why can't Dracula get a girlfriend?

Because he has bat breath!

How can you tell if there's a monster in your fridge?

You can't shut the door.

What happens when monsters
enter a beauty contest?

They get disqualified for
being too ugly.

Monster boy: "Is that your real face
or are you wearing a gas-mask?"

Monster girl: "I didn't come here to
be insulted."

Boy: "Oh, where do you normally go?"

How do monsters count
to thirteen?

On their fingers.

How do monsters count to 47?

They take off their socks and count
their toes.

Why did the monster
cross the road?

He wanted some
chicken for his tea.

What do you get if you
cross a Scottish monster
with a hamburger?

A Big Mac.

What weighed twenty stone
and terrorised Paris?

The Fat-tum of the Opera.

Girl monster: "I wish I had a pound
for every boy that has asked me
to marry him."

Boy monster: "What would you
buy, a bag of crisps?"

What do demons have on holiday?

A devil of a time.

Why are monsters big and hairy?

So you can tell them apart from gooseberries.

Monster brother: "Don't look out of the window you'll confuse people."

Monster sister: "What do you mean?"

Monster Brother: "They'll think Hallowe'en is early this year."

What happened when a purple-headed monster took up singing?

He had a frog in his throat.

What happened when two huge monsters ran in a race?

One ran in short bursts, the other ran in burst shorts.

Why was the demon so good at cooking?

He was a kitchen devil.

How did the midget monster get into the police force?

He lied about his height.

Did you hear the joke about the two monsters who crashed?

They fell off a cliff, boom! boom!

When do banshees howl?

On Moanday night.

Monster 1: "I have a hunch."

Monster 2: "I thought you were a funny shape."

How do you get six monsters in a biscuit tin?

Take the biscuits out first.

Did you hear about the man who took up monster-baiting for a living?

He used to be a teacher but he lost his nerve.

How do you talk
to a giant?

Use big words.

A little demon
came running into the
house saying "Mum, Dad's
fallen on the bonfire."

"Great" said Mum, "we'll have
a barbecue!"

What did the monster get
when he multiplied 497 by 684?

The wrong answer.

What did the little demon do when
he bought a house?

He called it Gnome Sweet Gnome.

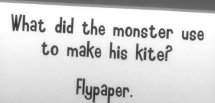

What did the monster use
to make his kite?

Flypaper.

What happened when the nasty
monster went shoplifting?

He stole a free sample.

What happened when the big, black
monster became a chimney sweep?

He started a grime wave.

What happened when a
monster fell in love
with a grand piano?

He said, "Darling, you've
got lovely teeth."

What has 2,000 eyes and 4,000 feet?

1,000 monsters.

What do you call a mammoth who conducts an orchestra?

Tuskanini.

What can a monster do that you can't do?

Count up to 25 on his fingers.

What is the difference between a huge, smelly monster and a sweet?

People like sweets!

Why
do monsters
wear glasses?

So they don't bump into
other monsters.

 When are monsters green?

When they don't take their
travel sickness pills.

Why did the monster knit
herself three socks?

Because she grew another foot.

How
do you communicate with
the Loch Ness Monster at
20,000 fathoms?

Drop him a line!

How do you keep an ugly monster in suspense?

I'll tell you tomorrow!

How do you know if a monster has come around for tea?

There are muddy footprints on the carpet!

What do you get if you cross a dinosaur with a wizard?

A Tyrannosaurus hex.

What did the monster want to eat in the restaurant?

The finger bowl.

Did you hear about the Irish monster who went to night school to learn to read in the dark?

What do you call a team of vultures playing football?

Foul play.

What did the werewolf write on his Christmas cards?

Best vicious of the season.

What happened to the wolf that fell into the washing machine?

It became a wash and werewolf.

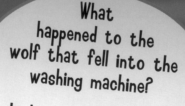

What do you call a hairy beast that no longer exists?

A were-wolf.

Where do vampires go on holiday?

The Isle of Fright.

Who speaks at the ghosts' press conference?

The spooksperson!

"Mummy, Mummy, kids at school say I look like a werewolf!"

"Don't worry about that, darling, now comb your face."

What do you get if you cross a hairdresser with a werewolf?

A monster with an all-over perm.

Why do werewolves do well at school?

Because every time they're asked a question, they come up with a snappy answer.

What do you call a hairy beast in a river?

A weir-wolf.

How do you know that a werewolf's been in the fridge?

There are paw prints in the butter.

What do you call two witches that share a room?

Broom mates!

Did you hear about the sick werewolf?

He lost his voice but is howl right now.

What do you get if you cross a witch with a werewolf?

A mad dog that chases aeroplanes.

Did you hear about the comedian who entertained at a werewolves' party?

He had them howling in the aisles.

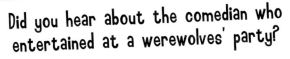

Why did the Mum and Dad werewolves call their son Camera?

Because he was always snapping.

Why shouldn't you grab a werewolf by its tail?

It might be the werewolf's tail, but it could be the end of you.

Why did the witch put her broom in the washing machine?

She wanted a clean sweep.

How does a witch tell the time?

With a witch watch!

What is a
ghost's favourite
dessert?

Boo-berry pie with
I-scream!

What
noise does a witch's
breakfast cereal make?

Snap, cackle and pop!

What happens if you cross a
werewolf with a sheep?

You have to get a new sheep.

What do you get if you cross a
ghost with a packet of crisps?

Snacks that go crunch in the night.

What do you think of Dracula films?

Fangtastic!

Why are ghosts cowards?

Because they've got no guts!

Why do dragons sleep during the day?

So they can fight knights.

What do Red Indian ghosts sleep in?

A creepy teepee!

What
did the mother ghost
say to the baby ghost?

Put your boos and
shocks on.

How do you make a milkshake?

Sneak up behind a glass of milk
and yell "Boo."

When do ghosts usually appear?

Just before someone screams.

Why are skeletons usually so calm?

Nothing gets under their skin!

What story do little witches like to hear at bedtime?

Ghoul deluxe and the three scares!

What do you call a witch's motorbike?

A brooooooooom stick!

Why do skeletons hate winter?

Because the cold goes right through them!

What do vampires gamble with?

Stake money!

What do you call an old and foolish vampire?

A silly old sucker!

Why did dinosaurs have wrinkles in their knees?

They stayed in the swimming pool too long.

Why does a monster climb a tree?

To get to its nest.

Why do dinosaurs climb trees?

There's nothing else to climb in the jungle.

Why did the monster lie on his bed?

To trip up low-flying aircraft.

Why did the dinosaur cross the road?

Because there were no chickens in those days.

Why do monsters have flat feet?

They don't wear sneakers.

How can you tell if a monster is visiting your house?

His tricycle will be parked outside.

Why does a monster have cracks between his toes?

To carry his credit cards.

Why don't more monsters join the police force?

They can't hide behind billboards.

Where is the monster's temple?

On the other side of his head.

What weighs 100 pounds, is grey and flies?

A 100-pound monster bird.

Why do monsters ride bikes?

To get to work.

Why did the monster walk on two legs?

To give the ants a chance.

What's red on the outside and green on the inside?

A monster wearing red pyjamas.

Why did the monster lie on his back in the water and stick his feet up?

So you could tell he wasn't a bar of soap.

What are monsters' favourite snacks?

Monster Munch.

Why do monsters have long toenails on Friday?

Because they don't have a pedicure until Saturday.

What did the man say when he saw a monster coming down the path wearing sunglasses?

Nothing, he didn't recognise him.

Why didn't the monster cross the road?

Because he didn't want to be mistaken for a chicken!

What is worse than a monster on waterskis?

A porcupine on a rubber life raft!

Why do monsters hide in the strawberry patch?

They like strawberries.

Why are most monsters green?

So they can hide in the bushes.

Why don't monsters take ballet lessons?

Because they grow out of their leotards quickly.

What did ET's mother say to him when he got home?

"Where on Earth have you been?"

Monster 1: "I am so thirsty my tongue is hanging out!"

Monster 2: "Oh, I thought it was your tie."

Where do ghouls go to study?

Ghoullege.

How does a monster get down from a tree?

He sits on a leaf and waits for autumn.

What do you do if you find yourself surrounded by monsters?

Hope that you are having a nightmare!

Why did the monster take his nose apart?

To see what made it run.

What do you call a dead monster?

Nothing, he can't hear you.

What did one of Frankenstein's ears say to the other?

I didn't know that we were living on the same block!

How does a monster climb a tree?

He sits on a seed and waits for it to grow.

Who does a monster ask for a date?

Any old ghoul he can find.

Did you hear about the brainless monster that sat on the floor?

He fell off.

Why did the monster jump up and down?

Because he had just taken his medicine and had forgotten to shake the bottle.

Frankenstein decided to build an extension to his laboratory, so he crossed a cement mixer, a ghoul and a chicken. Now he's got a demon brick layer.

What do you give a nervous mammoth?

Trunquilizers.

Why do monsters live in jungles?

It's cheaper than renting a house.

What has two heads, five hands, a nose and six feet?

A monster with spare parts.

Why are vampires artistic?

They are good at drawing blood.

What do you get if you cross a monster with a cat?

A very large mouse catcher who messes up your house with big paw prints.

What is big, green and loves curry?

An Indian monster.

What comes out at night and goes munch, munch, ouch?

A vampire with a rotten tooth.

Why do monsters lie down?

Because they can't lie up.

Is it hard to bury a dead monster?

Yes, it's a huge undertaking.

What did the dragon say when he saw St George in his shining armour?

Oh no, not more tinned food.

What did the traffic light say to the monster?

Don't look now, I'm changing.

How many monsters can you get in a car?

Four. Two in the front and two in the back.

Which side of a monster has the most skin?

The outside.

Why shouldn't you dance with a monster?

Because you will end up with flat feet!

Why did the monster wear red shoes?

His blue ones were at the cobblers.

Where are monsters found?

They're so big they're hardly ever lost!

How did the monster double his money?

He folded it in half.

Monster 1: "Have you ever had trouble with appendicitis?"

Monster 2: "Only when I tried to spell it."

Do monsters always snore?

No, only when they are asleep.

How do you get a
monster in your car?

Open the door.

Why
do monsters live
in forests?

Because they are too big
to live in houses!

What looks like half
a monster?

The other half.

Did you hear about the spook
that lived on a high-fibre diet?

He lived on beans and ghost
twice a day.

What do you call a
monster in the desert?

Lost.

Why
did the ghost's trousers
fall down?

Because he had no visible
means of support.

What do ghosts
like about horse riding?

Ghoulloping.

What do you get if you cross
a monster with a cat?

A creature that will get stuck
in the cat flap.

Why
did the monster chase
his own tail?

He was trying to make both
ends meet.

What happened when the
monster went to the flea circus?

He stole the show.

Why did the ghost hold a seance?

To try to contact the living.

What did the ghost estate agent say
to the ghost?

"Sorry sir, but we have nothing suitable
for you to haunt at the moment!"

How does a vampire enter his house?

Through the bat flap.

Which weight do ghosts box at?

Phantom weight.

How do you tell a good monster from a bad one?

If it's a good one, you will be able to talk about it later!

What happens when an Egyptian mummy eats biscuits in bed?

You get a crummy mummy.

What do you give
a monster with big feet?

Big shoes.

Monster 1: "Am I late for dinner?"

Monster 2: "Yes, everyone has
been eaten."

How does a monster
catch a squirrel?

He hides up a tree and
pretends to be a nut.

How can you tell if a vampire has been
at the tomato juice?

By the teeth marks on the carton.

If a boxer was knocked out by Dracula, what would he be?

Out for the Count.

What do you get if you cross a mole with a monster?

Very big holes in your garden.

What do you call a skeleton that is always telling lies?

A boney foney.

What do you call a monster in a revolving door?

Stuck.

What do you get if you cross
a midget with Dracula?

A vampire that sucks blood from
your knee caps.

What do skeletons say
before they begin dinner?

Bone appetit!

Why did King Kong paint the
bottoms of his feet brown?

So he could hide in the
peanut butter jar.

What
do you get if King Kong
falls down a mine shaft?

A flat miner.

What do you call a Scottish sea monster who hangs people?

The Loch Noose Monster.

What's brown and furry on the inside and clear on the outside?

King Kong in a fish tank.

What aftershave do monsters wear?

Brutel.

What do you do if you find King Kong in the kitchen?

Just don't monkey with him.

Why did King Kong join the army?

He wanted to find out about gorilla warfare.

Why did the Abominable Snowman send his father to Siberia?

He wanted an Ice Pop!

What's big, furry, dangerous and has four wheels?

A monster driving a car.

What's green and moves at a hundred miles an hour?

A monster jet.

What
do you call a
fat Jack-o-Lantern?

A plumpkin.

What makes a good
present for a monster?

Five pairs of gloves (one
for each hand).

Why did the monster
wear black boots?

Because his brown
ones were all muddy!

What
do monsters have that
no other animals have?

Baby monsters!

Which monsters
have the shortest legs?

The smallest ones!

How do you stop a dinosaur
from biting his nails?

Pull his foot out of his mouth.

What is Transylvania's
national sport?

Drac racing.

What
kind of monsters can be
found outside in the rain?

Drizzly monsters.

What did the monster say
when it laid a square egg?

"Ouch."

What do monkey-eating monsters eat
for dessert?

Chocolate chimp cookies.

How does a monster
get out of a small car?

The same way that he got in!

Did you hear what happened to
the vampire couple?

They love in vein.

What do you call a thirsty dinosaur?

Dry-serotops.

What's green and goes around and around?

A monster in a washing machine!

What's the favourite food of a fire-spitting monster?

Dragon Wheels.

Why did the monster eat candles?

For light refreshment.

What did the monster say to his psychiatrist?

"I feel abominable."

Why is the sky so high?

So monsters don't bump their heads.

Did you hear about the vain monster who was going bald?

The doctor couldn't do a hair transplant for him, so he shrunk his head to fit his hair.

What did the doctor say to the invisible monster's wife?

"I can't see anything wrong with your husband."

What do they have for lunch at Monster School?

Human beans, boiled legs, pickled bunions and eyes-cream.

Why are there fences around cemeteries?

Because people are dying to get in.

What do you get when you cross a man-eating monster's path?

Eaten!

How do you make a monster float?

Take two scoops of ice-cream, a glass of Coke and add one monster.

What animal did the monster become when he caught a cold?

A little hoarse!

What is a man-eating monster's favourite take-away meal?

Chinese Chow-man!

Why don't monsters eat penguins?

Because they can't get the wrappers off.

What's a monster's favourite play?

Romeo and Ghouliet.

What's big, red and has four wheels?

A monster in a Mini.

Why was the horrible, big monster making a terrible noise all night?

After eating Madonna he thought he could sing.

What has webbed feet, feathers, fangs and goes quack, quack?

Count Duckula.

What tools were used by carpenter dinosaurs?

Dino-saws.

What performers do vampires enjoy most at the circus?

The jugulars!

What sort of soup do monsters like?

One with plenty of body in it.

What do you get when you cross a black cat with a lemon?

Sour-puss.

What do yetis eat on top of Everest?

High tea.

129

What is the hardest
thing to sell a mummy?

Life insurance.

What is a monster's
favourite type of joke?

A tall story.

Did you hear about the very well-behaved
little monster?

When he was good, his father would give
him a penny and a pat on the head.

By the time he was sixteen he had £25 in
the bank and his head was totally flat!

What goes moan, moan, bang?

A moaning monster in a mine field.

What
do you get when you
cross Bambi with a ghost?

Bamboo.

What do you get when you
cross a snowman with a vampire?

Frostbite.

What do you call a prehistoric
creature that gets runs in cricket?

A dino-score.

What dinosaur was made of rocks?

Tyrannosaurus rocks!

What goes
moan, moan bang?

A moaning monster
in a mine field.

Why
did the dinosaur climb onto
the roof of the restaurant?

Because they advertised a free
meal on the house.

What do you get if you
cross a monster with a goat?

A dirty kid that scares people away.

What is at the top of a
Triceratop's legs?

A tricerabottom.

What
did the weigh-in
machine say when a
monster stood on it?

One at a time please.

What do you get if you cross
a monster with a hyena?

A gigglemonster.

What prehistoric monster went
down the yellow brick road?

The Lizard of Oz!

What do you call a superb
painting done by a monster?

A monsterpiece!

Why did mammoth cars have big trunks?

Because glove compartments hadn't been invented.

What is a monster's favourite card game?

Snap.

Monster 1: "Do you wake up miserable in the mornings?"

Monster 2: "No, I always let her sleep in."

What happens when a ghost haunts a theatre?

The actors get stage fright.

What do you call being frightened of a monster?

Sensible.

What goes ha, ha, ha, ha, plop?

A monster laughing its head off.

Why did the stupid monster take a tape measure to bed?

He wanted to see how long he slept.

What goes clomp, clomp, clomp, squish?

A monster with a wet shoe.

What animals use nutcrackers?

Toothless monsters.

What do you call the divorced wife of a Tyrannosaurus?

Tyrannosaurus's ex.

What's the difference between a monster and peas?

You can't mush monsters.

How do you stop a monster from messing up the house?

Put it in the garden.

Where do you find most monsters?

Between the head and the tail.

Why did the boy take an aspirin after hearing a werewolf howl?

Because it gave him an eerie ache.

What do you call a female monster with a piano on her head?

Joanna.

Did you hear about the monster that ate all the apples on the tree?

It died of apple-plexiti!

What did one ghost say to the other ghost?

"Do you believe in people?"

What do you get if you cross a sheepdog, a monster and a flower?

A monster collie-flower!

What did the dad ghost say to his family when driving?

Fasten your sheet belts.

What kind of monster chases anything red?

A monster bull!

What did the monster and
the history professor do?

They got together and
talked over old times.

What did the monster
do when he broke his toe?

He called a tow truck.

Two monsters were
running across the top
of a cereal packet.

"Why are we running so
fast?" asked one.

"Because it says 'Tear
along the dotted line!'"

How can you tell a
monster from a tomato?

The tomato is red.

What's big and ugly and found at twenty fathoms?

A monster with an aqualung.

What happens to a monster that keeps eating bits off the table?

He gets splinters in his mouth!

What is green, large and hums?

A dead monster.

How does a vampire travel?

In a blood vessel.

If a monster crosses a road, rolls in the mud on the other side and crosses back again, what is he?

A dirty double-crosser.

What is the difference between a hungry monster and a greedy monster?

One longs to eat and the other eats far too long.

What did the baby porcupine monster say when he backed into a cactus?

"Is that you, Mum?"

What do you get if you cross a mammoth with a skunk?

I don't know, but it wouldn't get a seat in the cinema.

What do you get if you cross a monster with a parrot?

Not sure, but I will certainly listen if it starts to speak.

What do you call a legless monster?

Anything you like. He can't chase you!

When a baby monster cries at night, who gets up?

The whole town.

Mrs Monster: "Will I lose my looks as I get older?"

Mr Monster: "I certainly hope so!"

What carries hundreds of giant needles but never sews?

A monster hedgehog.

What is the difference between a dead bee and a sick monster?

One is a seedy beast and the other's a bee deceased.

What prehistoric creature lived on the beach?

A dino-shore.

What is smaller than a monster's mouth?

Anything it eats.

What do you get if
you cross a mammoth
with a mouse?

A trunk full of cheese.

What is green, lumpy and
weighs eight tonnes?

A monster with mumps.

Which monsters are the snootiest?

The ones that live in trees (they look
down on all the other monsters).

What
would you get if you
crossed a pigeon, a frog and a
prehistoric animal?

A pigeon-toad dinosaur.